CLOSE TO HOME

52 Devotions to Build Character in Your Children

BONNIE BRUNO

Chariot Books™
David C. Cook Publishing Co.

Chariot Books™ is an imprint of David C. Cook Publishing Co.
David C. Cook Publishing Co., Elgin, Illinois 60120
David C. Cook Publishing Co., Weston, Ontario
Nova Distribution Ltd., Newton Abbot, England

CLOSE TO HOME: FIFTY-TWO DEVOTIONS TO BUILD CHARACTER IN YOUR CHILDREN
© 1993 by Bonnie Bruno for text and Wende Caporale for illustrations

Scripture quotations are from The Living Bible, © 1971, Tyndale House Publishers, Wheaton, IL 60187. Used by permission.

Designed by Elizabeth Thompson
First Printing, 1993
Printed in the United States of America
97 96 95 94 93 5 4 3 2 1

Library of Congress Cataloging-in-Pulbication Data
Bruno, Bonnie.
Close to Home : fifty-two devotions to build character in your children / by Bonnie Bruno.
p. cm.
ISBN 0-7814-0925-X
1. Family—Prayer-books and devotions—English. I. Title.
BV225.B78   1993
249—dc20   93-22187
                                                                                                    CIP

Contents ▲▲▲▲▲▲▲▲▲▲

# Using This Book

There are tremendous benefits to having family devotions. A life that pleases God is built gradually, one choice at a time. But it takes a plan—and time with the Master Builder.

Successful family devotions generally have three components:

1. Creating a habit of meeting with God.
2. Using concise, interesting, age-appropriate material.
3. Following through on what is learned.

Close to Home has been designed to meet these requirements for families with children aged three to eight.

Simple Steps to Follow

1. Make a date with your family members to work through *Close to Home*. Because these are once-a-week devotionals, you will probably be able to find one time each week when the whole family can be together for a brief time with God. The devotionals are not tied to Sunday—or any day. However, consider doing them on the same day each week so that they become part of your weekly routine. Any time of the day would be fine. Some families choose to meet together right after dinner.

2. Select a devotional. For convenience, you'll probably cover the devotionals in the order they appear. However, the studies can be done in any order and at any pace. Each devotional covers one of thirty-three qualities, such as commitment, forgiveness, cooperation, respectfulness, and compassion. The topics are listed with the corresponding study in the table of contents. If you see the need for more of a specific character quality in your home, you may want to cover that devotional sooner than it appears in the book.

   You don't have to wait for January 1 to begin *Close to Home* because the devotionals are not dated. The studies appropriate for the Easter, Thanksgiving, and Christmas seasons appear at the end of the book.

3. Familiarize yourself with the study ahead of time so that you can make the best use of your time together. Gather any materials needed. The only section that might require materials is "Try This!" and that will happen rarely. In

fact, because the Scripture is written out in each study, you can take the book anywhere you wish. Stories 7, 22, 24, 34, and 48 have outdoor themes, and hearing them in God's creation might enhance your time together.

An Overview

Each devotional is divided into the same five sections. Here's a brief description of the format and purpose of each section.

• **Story:** The story is meant to capture attention and stimulate discussion. Children who are good readers can take turns reading the stories aloud.

• **What Do You Think?** The three to five questions in this section bring home the message of the story. An adult will need to lead the discussion.

• **What Does the Bible Say?** This section contains a memorable Scripture passage and a few discussion questions. Using the discussion questions, try to determine how obeying Scripture could help the character in the story and your family live God's way. Seeing the value of the Scripture passage can motivate your family to memorize all or a simplified version of the verse.

• **Talking with God:** This section gives a simple prayer to build on.

• **Try This!** The optional follow-up activities vary in length and reinforce the message one step further. Some could take a few minutes right after your study; some, a day or an evening. Still others are ongoing projects (such as saving items to send to a missionary).

Building your child's character is a gradual but important process. And as the apostle Paul reminds us, we can do our part, but ultimately God is responsible for the growth that occurs (I Corinthians 3:7). Trust Him to multiply your efforts. It is my prayer that your times with God using *Close to Home* will draw you closer to Him and have a long-lasting impact on your family.

1 One Cookie, Two Friends

Teresa was sitting on her front porch.

"Hi, Teresa," called her friend Mary. "Want to come over to my house for a while?"

"Maybe later," Teresa called back. "I'm eating lunch right now."

Mary bounded up the porch steps. "I can wait!"

She sat down next to Teresa.

"What's in the bag?" she asked, craning her neck to see.

"The rest of my lunch," answered Teresa.

Teresa reached in and pulled out an orange, a small bag of carrot sticks, and one huge oatmeal cookie.

"Mmm-mm!" said Mary, licking her lips. "Looks delicious!"

Teresa ate the juicy orange. She munched on the crisp carrot sticks.

Then she glanced at Mary, who was staring like a hungry pup at the oatmeal cookie.

What Do You Think?

1. What do you suppose Mary was thinking?
2. Is it ever okay not to share? Why or why not?
3. Have you shared anything with a friend this week? Tell about it.

What Does the Bible Say?

And all the believers met together constantly and shared everything with each other. Acts 2:44

1. How could remembering Acts 2:44 help Teresa decide what to do about the cookie?
2. When could Acts 2:44 help you, too?
3. Memorize all or part of Acts 2:44.

Talking with God

Help me, dear God, to be willing to share with others. Amen.

Try This!

Schedule a family brownie baking event one Saturday soon. Bake enough of your favorite recipe to share with next-door neighbors.

2 Mom's Rule

Gary and Jason were racing home from the bus stop.

"I'm tired!" Gary said breathlessly. He tossed his schoolbooks on the front lawn and lay down beside them.

Jason plopped down next to him.

"Want to come inside?" asked Gary. "We could play my new video game and have something to drink."

"I can't," answered Jason with a shrug. "I'm supposed to ask Mom before I go to anyone's house."

"Why?" asked Gary.

"She likes to know where I am, that's all," explained Jason.

Gary rolled his eyes. "Well, I'm your best friend, remember? She knows you're safe here!"

"I know," agreed Jason, "but how will she even know I'm here if I don't tell her?"

Gary opened the door. "Well, I'm going inside now. Are you coming or not?"

What Do You Think?

1. What do you suppose Jason did?
2. Why is it important to let your mom or dad know where you are?
3. Have you ever forgotten to ask before visiting a friend's house? What happened?

What Does the Bible Say?

Children, obey your parents; this is the right thing to do because God has placed them in authority over you. Ephesians 6:1

1. How could remembering Ephesians 6:1 help Jason stand up to Gary?
2. When could Ephesians 6:1 help you, too?
3. Memorize Ephesians 6:1.

Talking with God

Dear God, help me to obey my family's rules willingly. Amen.

Try This!

Have each family member think of an important family rule. What would your home be like without these rules? What if everyone ignored the rules?

3 One Way to Win

A big red question mark covered Mrs. Bonner's classroom chalkboard.

"Boys and girls," she said, "this question mark represents a secret number that only our school principal, Mr. Carter, knows."

"What's the secret number for?" asked Jeff.

"The class that guesses closest to the secret number wins one hundred dollars. The money will be used to buy flowers to plant around our new school building."

The classroom buzzed with excitement. Planting flowers would be a fun project.

"Any leftover money can be used for a class party," Mrs. Bonner added with a grin. The class shrieked their approval.

Jeff had a secret of his own. He knew where Mr. Carter kept his secret information. He had watched him slide important pieces of paper into his bottom left desk drawer.

If I could take a quick peek in that drawer, thought Jeff, *our class could win the hundred dollars for sure.*

What Do You Think?

1. What do you think Jeff did?
2. Which is better: being honest, or winning a contest? Why?
3. How do you feel when you play fair even though you know a way to win by cheating?
4. Would you enjoy winning a contest by cheating? Why or why not?

What Does the Bible Say?

The Lord hates cheating and delights in honesty.
Proverbs 11:1

1. How could remembering Proverbs 11:1 help Jeff decide what to do?
2. When could Proverbs 11:1 help you, too?
3. Memorize Proverbs 11:1.

Talking with God

Thank You, Lord, for helping me make honest choices.
Amen.

Try This!

Buy a hearty flowering bush to plant together in your yard. (If you prefer an indoor plant, select a potted flower that will bloom on a windowsill.) Discuss the importance of honesty, comparing the results of each honest choice to a beautiful blossom opening up. Your special bush or potted plant will be a valuable reminder of your family's commitment to following God's path.

4 The Meanest Girl in Town

Kaitlin was helping her mom shop for groceries one afternoon.

"Choose seven or eight red apples," said Mom. "I'll get some bananas."

Kaitlin selected the shiniest red apples she could find. But as she turned away from the fruit display, she heard a sudden PLOP! followed by another and another.

PLOP! PLOP-PLOP! PLOP! One by one, apples fell like rocks rolling down a hillside.

"How stupid can you get?" hollered a familiar voice.

There stood Annie, a loudmouthed classmate who was always trying to get Kaitlin in trouble.

Kaitlin's face turned as red as the apples. *I ought to teach her a lesson and embarrass her back,* she thought.

What Do You Think?

1. What would you say if you were Kaitlin?
2. Do you know anyone like Annie?
3. How do you think you'd feel if you embarrassed someone on purpose?

What Does the Bible Say?

Don't repay evil for evil. Don't snap back at those who say unkind things about you. Instead, pray for God's help for them, for we are to be kind to others, and God will bless us for it. I Peter 3:9

1. How could remembering I Peter 3:9 help Kaitlin decide what to do?
2. When could I Peter 3:9 help you, too?
3. Memorize all or part of I Peter 3:9.

Talking with God

Dear God, please help me to be extra patient with those who try to hurt my feelings. Amen.

Try This!

Think of someone who reminds you of Annie. Every morning when you wake up, ask God to bless that person. (It might feel strange at first to pray for someone you do not like very well.) Praying for our "enemies" helps us set aside our anger and feel compassion for them.

5 A Pigful of Pennies

Chad and his sister Beth charged into the house.

"The circus is coming!" squealed Chad.

"It'll be here Saturday," Beth told Mother. "I can hardly wait!"

Mother was not smiling, though. "I'm sorry," she said quietly, "but we don't have the extra money right now. I'm afraid circus tickets are just too expensive for our budget this month."

Chad's face fell to his feet.

Beth moaned.

Then she had an idea. "Chad," she whispered, "come with me."

On the piano in the family room sat a pink piggy bank. The bank was filled to the top with pennies.

Chad and Beth had worked hard to save so much money. The pennies were supposed to go to the Jones family, who were serving as missionaries in Brazil.

"We could use the pennies for the circus and then fill it up again later," said Beth.

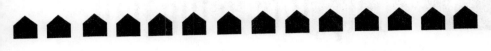

What Do You Think?

1. What do you suppose Chad and Beth decided to do?
2. What do you think about Beth's idea?
3. Have you ever promised to save for something important, then used the money for something else? What happened?

What Does the Bible Say?

If you want to know what God wants you to do, ask him, and he will gladly tell you. James 1:5a

1. How could remembering James 1:5a help Chad and Beth decide what to do?
2. When could James 1:5a help you, too?
3. Memorize all or part of James 1:5a.

Talking with God

Dear Lord, help me to make wise decisions that please You. Amen.

Try This!

Spend a few minutes discussing the importance of saving. Then, over the next few months, fill a small shipping box with helpful items for a missionary family (stationery, stamps, small toys, spice mixes, lotion, etc.). The missions committee at your church should be able to suggest a missionary family, their specific needs, and importing restrictions.

6 Footprints in the Hall

Sarah found a shortcut home from the park. The trail wound over a hill and around a small pond, right to her backyard gate.

One day after playing, Sarah darted into the house without thinking. She ran to her room to change clothes.

"I'm home," she called.

"I can see that," answered Mom. "There are muddy footprints across the kitchen and down the hall."

"No way," protested Sarah. "They can't be mine. I've been at the playground all morning, and it wasn't a bit muddy there."

"Sarah, check your shoes," said Mom. "These footprints match your sneakers."

Sarah studied each footprint. They were her size, all right. But the last thing she felt like doing was mopping up a muddy mess.

What Do You Think?

1. What do you think Sarah said next?
2. Why is it sometimes hard to admit our mistakes?
3. Can you think of a time when it was hard to say, "I'm sorry. It was my fault"? What happened?
4. What would the world be like if nobody ever said, "I'm sorry"?

What Does the Bible Say?

A man who refuses to admit his mistakes can never be successful. Proverbs 28:13a

1. How could remembering Proverbs 28:13a help Sarah decide what to do?
2. When could Proverbs 28:13a help you, too?
3. Memorize Proverbs 28:13a.

Talking with God

Help me, dear God, to apologize for my goofs even when I don't feel like it. Amen.

Try This!

As a family, make a poster that celebrates God's forgiveness. When we confess our mistakes, He is faithful to forgive us every time.

Search for verses that can be used on the poster. Hang up the poster as a reminder that we all need to ask God and others for forgiveness.

7 The Rainbow Garden

Mr. Miller was a white-haired man who lived on the corner near Allen's house. Mr. Miller reminded Allen of his own grandpa.

Whenever Allen rode his bike to the corner to turn around, Mr. Miller would wave to him. Every time he walked to the store, Mr. Miller would ask him what he was up to.

But one afternoon, Mr. Miller was nowhere to be found.

Allen stuck his head inside Mr. Miller's back gate. "Mr. Miller, are you okay?" he called gingerly.

"Sure am! Come on in!" Mr. Miller called back.

He threw Allen a bright smile and continued with his work. "I'm planting a rainbow garden," said Mr. Miller. "Wildflowers. Would you like to grab a packet of flower seeds and help?"

Allen thought of his favorite game show on TV. He thought about his puppy, Harriet, who would be waiting for him to get home from the store. But most of all he thought about the popcorn that he'd planned to pop when he got home.

What Do You Think?

1. Do you think Allen stayed to help Mr. Miller? Do you think Allen was pleased with his decision?
2. What kind of a neighbor does Mr. Miller seem to be?
3. Tell of a time when someone stopped everything to help you.

What Does the Bible Say?

Let everyone see that you are unselfish and considerate in all you do. Philippians 4:5a

1. How could remembering Philippians 4:5a help Allen decide what to do?
2. When could Philippians 4:5a help you, too?
3. Memorize Philippians 4:5a.

Talking with God

Thank You, God, for always being there to help me. Amen.

Try This!

Do you know a senior adult in your neighborhood? Would he or she appreciate some help with yard work or gardening? Check your calendar and set aside some time to help that person. Your family might be God's answer to his or her prayer.

8 One Tiny Fib

It was Saturday—cleanup day. Joe was raking the yard while Dad trimmed the bushes.

"Pile the leaves over there in the corner, son," said Dad. "We're going to start a compost pile."

Joe filled the wheelbarrow seven times. The pile in the corner soon turned into a huge mound of golden leaves.

"How's it going?" called Dad.

Joe paused to wipe his sweaty forehead. "Okay," he called back, "I'm almost finished."

Dad gave him the thumbs-up sign.

The last load of leaves was going to be small. So small, in fact, that it was hardly worth the effort it would take to haul it across the yard.

Joe sat on the grass next to the wheelbarrow and sighed. If he just spread the leaves around the yard with his rake, Dad would probably figure they'd fallen off the tree after the work was finished.

One tiny fib won't hurt, thought Joe.

What Do You Think?

1. What do you suppose Joe decided to do?
2. Is there really such a thing as a "tiny" fib?
3. Have you ever felt like telling a lie because you were tired?
4. Can you really trust someone who lies to you?

What Does the Bible Say?

Work hard and with gladness all the time, as though working for Christ, doing the will of God with all your hearts. Ephesians 6:7

1. How could remembering Ephesians 6:7 help Joe make a wise choice?
2. When could Ephesians 6:7 help you, too?
3. Memorize all or part of Ephesians 6:7.

Talking with God

Help me, God, to be honest in all that I do. Amen.

Try This!

Play a "Who Am I?" game using Bible characters who are remembered for their honesty, such as Job, Paul, and Jesus. Discuss why honesty is pleasing to God.

9 Kathy's Promise

Kathy's best friend, Melissa, was gone for the weekend.

"What'll I do until Melissa gets back?" Kathy asked her mother.

"Well, how about having another friend overnight?" suggested Mother.

"Like Amy?" asked Kathy.

"Sure. Give her a call," said Mother.

Amy arrived at five o'clock. She and Kathy ate pizza and watched a funny movie on TV. When it was time for bed, they unrolled their sleeping bags and spread them on the living-room floor.

"I'll tell you a secret if you'll tell me one of yours, too," Amy whispered in the dark.

Kathy thought hard. The only real secret she knew was one that Melissa had made her promise never to tell.

"You go first," said Amy.

What Do You Think?

1. Do you think Kathy told her secret? What happened?
2. What would you do if a friend asked you to tell a secret?
3. Why is it important to keep secrets, anyway? What's the difference between telling your own secret and telling someone else's?
4. How do you suppose God feels about keeping secrets?

What Does the Bible Say?

A true friend is always loyal. Proverbs 17:17a

1. How could remembering Proverbs 17:17a help Kathy decide what to do?
2. When could Proverbs 17:17a help you, too?
3. Memorize Proverbs 17:17a.

Talking with God

Dear God, help me to be loyal to You by being loyal to my family and friends. Amen.

Try This!

Play several rounds of "gossip." Sit in a circle. One person whispers a sentence into the ear of the person to the left. The sentence goes around the circle until it reaches the last person, who says it out loud. (Usually the message ends up jumbled and makes little sense.)

Compare the game of "gossip" to what happens when people cannot control their tongues. Secrets are for keeping, not spreading carelessly.

25

10 The New Girl

The green house at the end of the street was getting a new family. Kerry, Tim, and Manuel skated up the sidewalk to investigate.

"Looks like they have kids," said Manuel, pointing to three bicycles and a skateboard.

"Looks like they have a dog, too," noted Kerry.

The front door swung open. A man from the moving company stepped outside, followed by a lady and her daughter.

"She looks about our age," whispered Tim. "Let's talk to her."

"No, not now," said Kerry. "She's probably busy."

"Yeah, so am I," Manuel said and skated away.

"But she doesn't have any friends yet," argued Tim.

"So what?" said Kerry, throwing up her hands. "She'll make friends at school tomorrow." And away she skated, too.

Tim leaned against a tree and watched the man carry in boxes. *It must feel awful to have no friends,* he thought.

What Do You Think?

1. Do you think Tim introduced himself to the new girl? What happened?

2. Have you ever been the new person in a situation? How did you feel?

3. Why do you suppose Kerry and Manuel were so unfriendly to their new neighbor?

4. What could Kerry, Manuel, and Tim have done to make the girl feel welcome?

What Does the Bible Say?

But if a person isn't loving and kind, it shows that he doesn't know God—for God is love. I John 4:8

1. How could remembering I John 4:8 help Kerry, Manuel, and Tim act the way God would want them to act?

2. When could I John 4:8 help you, too?

3. Memorize all or part of I John 4:8.

Talking with God

Dear Lord, help me to think of special ways to show Your kindness and love to others. Amen.

Try This!

Is there a new boy or girl in your neighborhood? at school? Get together with some friends and make a giant WELCOME! card to deliver.

11 Dana's Special Job

Everybody in Dana's family had a household chore to do.

Dad mowed the yard. Mom vacuumed the rugs every other day and did the laundry. Jamie set the table and filled the milk glasses for each meal. Dana fed their dog, Blackie, and made sure he had fresh water in his bowl.

One day Dana forgot to feed Blackie. She forgot to check his water bowl.

Poor Blackie trailed her from room to room, trying to get her attention. "I'm starving!" his sad eyes seemed to say.

But Dana was too busy to care. She talked on the phone to her friends, worked on spelling homework, and listened to a favorite tape. But late that night, Dana suddenly remembered Blackie. She knew she'd forgotten to feed him. She knew that his water bowl must surely be empty.

The house was dark and chilly. Dana pulled her warm quilt up to her chin. She pictured poor, hungry Blackie lying on his blanket in the garage.

What Do You Think?

1. Do you think Dana got out of bed and went to the garage to take care of Blackie? What happened?
2. What are some of your special jobs around the house?
3. What does the word *cooperation* mean? (Look it up in the dictionary if you aren't sure.)
4. Do you think Dana was cooperating with her family?

What Does the Bible Say?

The lazy man is full of excuses. Proverbs 22:13a

1. How could remembering Proverbs 22:13a help Dana act the way God would want her to act?
2. When could Proverbs 22:13a help you make wise choices?
3. Memorize Proverbs 22:13a.

Talking with God

Remind me, dear God, how important it is for me to do my jobs on time. Amen.

Try This!

Think of some important chores that must be done at your house. Take turns talking about what would happen if they were ignored. (Example: What if Mom quit cooking meals?)

12 Bobby's Fault

Jared lay in the hammock, reading a book.

"What's the book about?" asked his friend, Bobby.

"It's a mystery," muttered Jared, throwing Bobby one of his don't-bother-me looks.

Bobby tilted his head to read the book's title.

"*The Secret of the Lost Cave*," he said. "Sounds good. Can I borrow it when you're through?"

"I guess so," mumbled Jared. "But you'll have to take good care of it. I borrowed it from the library."

Jared finished the book in three days and then passed it along to Bobby. But when it was time to return the book to the library, Bobby still had four chapters to go.

One morning the librarian phoned Jared. "*The Secret of the Lost Cave* is nine days overdue," she informed him.

"Yes, I know," said Jared. "But it's Bobby's fault. He's kind of a slow reader."

"Well, Bobby may be a slow reader, but you will have to pay the fine promptly," said the librarian.

What Do You Think?

1. How do you think Jared reacted to the news?
2. Was it fair of Jared to blame the overdue book on Bobby? What part of the problem was Bobby's fault? What part was Jared's fault?
3. What would you say to someone who keeps forgetting to return what he or she has borrowed?
4. Why is it easier to blame someone else for our mistakes?

What Does the Bible Say?

Have two goals: wisdom—that is, knowing and doing right—and common sense. Proverbs 3:21

1. How could remembering Proverbs 3:21 help Jared understand his problem? What could he decide to do next time?
2. When could Proverbs 3:21 help you, too?
3. Memorize all or part of Proverbs 3:21.

Talking with God

Dear God, help me to accept responsibility for my actions. Amen.

Try This!

   Plan a family outing to the library. When you get home, make a list of all the books and tapes you borrowed, along with their due dates. Hang the list on the refrigerator door. And remember, each person is responsible for watching the calendar! Any overdue fines must be paid by the person who checked out that book or tape.

13 The Flyaway Word

It was Nancy's birthday.

"I'll tie balloons on the backyard fence," she told her parents.

"Don't forget to hang streamers from the trees," kidded Dad.

Nancy taped red, blue, and yellow balloons along the top of the fence. She draped purple crepe paper streamers between the posts.

"Looks like someone's getting ready for a party," called Mrs. Werner, the lady next door.

"Yes, it's my birthday," beamed Nancy.

"How many are coming to the party?" asked Mrs. Werner.

"Fifteen, counting me," said Nancy.

"Fifteen?" croaked Mrs. Werner. She looked like she'd swallowed a bee. "Well, just keep the noise down!"

"Grouch," Nancy mumbled.

"What's that, young lady?" said Mrs. Werner. "I didn't hear you."

What Do You Think?

1. Why do you think Nancy was so upset with Mrs. Werner?
2. Have you ever treated someone disrespectfully when you were angry?
3. Is there ever a good excuse for name-calling?
4. Do you think Nancy apologized to Mrs. Werner? What happened?

What Does the Bible Say?

The tongue is a small thing, but what enormous damage it can do. James 3:5a

1. How could remembering James 3:5a help Nancy act wisely?
2. When could James 3:5a help you, too?
3. Memorize James 3:5a.

Talking with God

Help me think before I speak, dear God, especially when I am upset. Amen.

Try This!

Can you think of a time when you wanted to "tell someone off" but didn't? What helped you control your tongue?

Think of ways to show more courtesy within your family. Have a time of sharing ideas.

14 The Hay Cake

Sam's sister baked a special treat on the last day of school.

"It's a celebration cake," she said proudly.

"But isn't it sort of lopsided, Deanna?" asked Sam.

"Well, that's because you kept opening the oven door while it was baking," frowned Deanna. "Anybody with half a brain knows not to do that."

Sam took a big bite of cake.

Deanna waited for him to say how delicious it was.

The cake was dry and springy. It reminded Sam of a mouthful of hay. He even felt the crunch of an eggshell between his teeth.

"Well, how is it?" asked Deanna.

What Do You Think?

1. Do you think Sam told Deanna the truth about her cake?
2. Do you know what tactfulness is? (Look it up in the dictionary if you aren't sure.) How could Sam have answered Deanna tactfully?
3. Have you ever made something special for someone who didn't appreciate it?

What Does the Bible Say?

Your own soul is nourished when you are kind.
Proverbs 11:17a

1. How could remembering Proverbs 11:17a help Sam decide what to do?
2. When could Proverbs 11:17a help you, too?
3. Memorize Proverbs 11:17a.

Talking with God

Dear God, please help me to choose my words carefully.
Amen.

Try This!

Think of several situations in which the use of tact would be helpful. Assign a situation to each family member, and let each one decide how he or she would handle it. If there's a "better" answer, remember to be tactful in your advice!

15 What's That Noise?

Juwhe could hardly wait to visit her friend, Dee. Dee's cat had given birth to five tiny kittens.

"Wear this special watch," said Mom. "When the alarm rings, you'll know it's time to come home."

Juwhe and Dee crouched at the door of a walk-in closet. They watched five hungry kittens nursing from their mother. Later, they saw them huddle together for a nap.

"Let's go up in my tree house while they're sleeping," suggested Dee.

Juwhe followed her friend up ten sturdy wooden stairs. They listened to the radio and played checkers high above the yard. They set bread crumbs on a nearby tree branch and watched a blackbird carry them away, one by one.

Bzzzz! Juwhe's alarm startled them both.

"What's that noise?" cried Dee.

Juwhe wanted to tell Dee to ignore the alarm. She certainly didn't feel like going home yet!

What Do You Think?

1. What do you suppose Juwhe did? What happened then?
2. Do you think the alarm was a good idea or not?
3. Have you ever gotten home late because you wanted to stay longer?
4. Why do parents always say to be home at a certain time?

What Does the Bible Say?

The Lord is fair in everything he does, and full of kindness.
Psalm 145:17

1. How could remembering Psalm 145:17 help Juwhe decide what to do?
2. When could Psalm 145:17 help you, too?
3. Memorize Psalm 145:17.

Talking with God

Help me, dear God, to understand the importance of rules
and to try my best to obey them. Amen.

Try This!

Have a silly time together writing imaginary rules for your parents.
(Examples: Always eat your cake before your vegetables. Only make your
bed on Wednesdays.)

Set aside a few minutes to talk about why parents need to set time
restrictions. In a way, RULE is another way to spell LOVE.

16 Just a Grape

Heidi loved to go grocery shopping with her mother at the new supermarket. Her favorite section was piled high with apples, oranges, pears, and grapes.

One day Heidi spotted a bin filled with her favorite green grapes.

"Let's get some of these for lunch," she suggested.

"Mmm, they do look good," agreed Mom, "except for the price. A dollar forty-nine per pound is too expensive for grapes."

Heidi's mouth watered. *Well, if they're too expensive to buy, I'll just try one,* she thought.

She waited for Mom to turn the corner near the potatoes. If she were quick, she'd be able to grab a grape and pop it into her mouth without anyone seeing.

It sounded so easy, and yet Heidi had a strange, nervous feeling in her stomach.

What Do You Think?

1. Do you think Heidi took a grape after all? What happened?
2. Why do you suppose she felt so uneasy?
3. Is there a difference between "trying" a grape without paying for it and stealing a bicycle?

What Does the Bible Say?

Keep me far from every wrong; help me, undeserving as I am, to obey your laws. Psalm 119:29

1. How could remembering Psalm 119:29 help Heidi decide what to do?
2. When could Psalm 119:29 help you, too?
3. Memorize all or part of Psalm 119:29.

Talking with God

Help me, dear God, to be honest even when no one is looking. Amen.

Try This!

Sit in a small circle. Tie the end of a ball of string to your wrist and begin a story about someone who is doing something dishonest. When you reach a decision point in the story, throw the ball of string to another family member. That person adds to the story then throws the ball of string to someone else, holding onto a piece of the string.

Repeat the process until the story reaches a logical ending point. Then look at the tangled string—the web of deceit that dishonest actions create.

17 I'll Do It

Ben had the whole room to himself for once. Randy, his brother, was spending the weekend with a friend.

"You can use my stereo if you'll clean the closet while I'm away," said Randy.

"Sure, I'll do it," said Ben. He'd do anything to get a chance at Randy's new stereo.

The weekend flew by. Ben spent Saturday hiking with his dad. After church on Sunday, he stopped to visit his grandparents.

When he arrived home, Ben kicked off his shoes. Music from Randy's stereo filled the room as he relaxed on the bed.

That's when he remembered his promise. "Sure, I'll do it," seemed to echo off the walls.

Ben peered into the messy closet and groaned. Slamming the doors shut, he promised himself he'd get to it later.

The clock showed that Randy would be home in one hour.

What Do You Think?

1. What do you think Ben did? Why?
2. Why was it easy for Ben to say, "I'll do it," but hard for him to get the job done?
3. Are promises for keeping only when we feel like it? Why?
4. Do you know someone who is dependable? What is it like to be with that person?

What Does the Bible Say?

If you wait for perfect conditions, you will never get anything done. Ecclesiastes 11:4

1. How could remembering Ecclesiastes 11:4 help Ben act responsibly?
2. When could Ecclesiastes 11:4 help you, too?
3. Memorize Ecclesiastes 11:4.

Talking with God

Dear God, remind me to put my promises first. Amen.

Try This!

Make "Because I Love You . . ." coupons for each member of your family. Promise to do a different chore each week, then be ready to fulfill that promise when the coupon is redeemed.

18 Matthew's Big Story

Matthew won the prize in his school's adventure-writing contest. Matthew's story was about a fishing trip he'd taken with his Uncle Al.

"No wonder I won! I wrote about the time I caught the biggest fish in the whole lake," he bragged. "In fact, nobody has seen a fish that big in the whole state!"

Matthew described how he baited the hook. "It was a special giant-sized worm that catches only giant fish," he said.

Matthew showed his prize-winning paper to everyone who would listen. "Pretty good, huh?" he'd ask.

That afternoon while Matthew was bragging, he ran into his friend, Syd. Syd's paper had not fared well in the contest.

"Can you believe it?" gushed Matthew. "I actually won the story contest."

Syd only glared back at Matthew.

What Do You Think?

1. Do you think Matthew apologized to Syd for bragging? What do you think happened?
2. Why is it important to think of others' feelings, too?
3. What is the difference between being proud of yourself and boasting?

What Does the Bible Say?

My protection and success come from God alone.
Psalm 62:7a

1. How could remembering Psalm 62:7a help Matthew act wisely?
2. When could Psalm 62:7a help you, too?
3. Memorize Psalm 62:7a.

Talking with God

Dear Lord, thank You for helping me to do my best. Please show me how to be proud without bragging to others. Amen.

Try This!

Take a few minutes to think of something nice to say about the other members of your family. Each person gets a turn to "brag" about everyone else.

19 Aunt Mae's Book

Aunt Mae loved to read. But sometimes she read too much—at least that's what Brenda thought.

"Let's catch some baby frogs," said Brenda one sunny afternoon.

"Sorry, hon," said Aunt Mae, peeking over her big book. "I'm reading right now. Maybe later."

Brenda shrugged. "You always say 'later,'" she grumbled.

After supper, Brenda asked Aunt Mae, "Is now a good time?"

"Sure," Aunt Mae answered cheerily. "I thought you'd never ask."

While they were catching baby frogs, Brenda asked Aunt Mae a question she'd been saving all day.

"Why are you always reading that book anyway? Won't you ever finish it?"

Aunt Mae laughed out loud. "It's my Bible," she explained, "and no, I'll probably never finish it."

Brenda had an idea. The next time Aunt Mae finished reading, she'd hide the book where she'd never find it again.

What Do You Think?

1. Do you think Brenda had a good idea? Why or why not?
2. Why do you suppose the Bible was so important to Aunt Mae?
3. Does anyone in your family read the Bible every day?
4. Why did Aunt Mae say that she'd never finish the Bible?

What Does the Bible Say?

Open my eyes to see wonderful things in your Word.
Psalm 119:18

1. How could understanding Psalm 119:18 help Brenda make a good choice?
2. When could Psalm 119:18 help you, too?
3. Memorize Psalm 119:18.

Talking with God

Dear God, help me to take time to appreciate Your Word.
Amen.

Try This!

See how many of the Bible memory verses you can repeat without help. Discuss ways to make memorizing God's Word easier to do.

20 Why Help a Grump?

Mike and his dad were walking across the store parking lot. They spotted a lady on crutches who was struggling to open the store's heavy door.

"Hey, isn't that Mrs. Parker?" asked Dad.

Everyone who waited for the school bus knew about grumpy Mrs. Parker. If she wasn't nagging the kids to stay away from her precious begonias, she was peering through her blinds to try and catch them dropping a gum wrapper.

"Pick up that trash this instant!" she would holler from her living-room window. Then she'd add a quick, "Or else!"

Mike watched Mrs. Parker balancing on one crutch while she tried to open the door. *I probably ought to help her,* he thought. *But why help a grump?*

What Do You Think?

1. What do you suppose Mike did? What was the result?
2. Why is it easy to help someone we like, but hard to offer help to someone who isn't very friendly to us?
3. Do you think Jesus would have helped Mrs. Parker?

What Does the Bible Say?

Whenever we can we should always be kind to everyone.
Galatians 6:10a

1. How could memorizing Galatians 6:10a help Mike make a good decision?
2. When could Galatians 6:10a help you, too?
3. Memorize Galatians 6:10a.

Talking with God

Dear heavenly Father, please give me a heart that's willing to overlook the faults of others. Amen.

Try This!

Think of someone in your neighborhood or church who may not have many pleasurable ways to occupy his or her time. Invite that person to share some time with your family.

21 Too Little, Too Big

Courtney was visiting her friend, Ruth, who lived across town. Courtney and Ruth had once been neighbors.

"Remember our clubhouse?" asked Ruth.

"Of course I remember," laughed Courtney. "My dad is the one who built it. And I remember how the other kids always told me I was 'too little' to be president."

"Want to see it?" asked Ruth. "It still looks the same."

Courtney followed Ruth through the woods behind Ruth's house. The smell of the damp trail brought back special memories.

There in a clearing sat a small, gray shed. When they arrived, it was already filled with giggling little girls.

Courtney knocked on the door and peeked inside.

"Hey!" hollered a ponytailed girl who sat near the door. "You're too big to join!"

Courtney's face turned crimson. She wanted to tell the girl that the clubhouse was built by *her* dad and that she could use it until she was a hundred and forty if she wanted to.

What Do You Think?

1. Why do you think Courtney was so upset?
2. Do you think she had a special right to the clubhouse?
3. Are there some things you are too big for now? How does that make you feel?

What Does the Bible Say?

There is a right time for everything. Ecclesiastes 3:1

1. How could remembering Ecclesiastes 3:1 help Courtney decide what to do?
2. When could Ecclesiastes 3:1 help you, too?
3. Memorize Ecclesiastes 3:1.

Talking with God

Dear Lord, help me to accept the changes that come with growing up. Thank You that I will never outgrow Your love. Amen.

Try This!

Have each family member describe two activities he or she liked at a much younger age, two things he or she enjoys now, and two things he or she dreams of being able to do someday.

22 Frozen Like a Statue

Sarah was afraid of spiders. If she saw one crawling across the sidewalk, she'd squash it. If she spotted a spider hanging on a web, she'd knock it down with Mom's big, yellow broom.

One summer morning during a camp-out, Sarah was gathering a pocketful of miniature pinecones. "I'm going to make a wreath with them," she told her sister, Shari.

Sarah turned to check under a tree to her right and was horrified to spot something brown and creepy sitting on her sleeve. The biggest, ugliest spider she had ever seen started making its way up her arm.

Sarah was so scared, she couldn't even scream. She was frozen like a statue, unable even to swat at the spider with her other hand.

What Do You Think?

1. Why do you think Sarah was so petrified of spiders?
2. Are you afraid of anything that small?
3. Can you think of a way for Sarah to overcome her fear of spiders?

What Does the Bible Say?

But when I am afraid, I will put my confidence in you.
Psalm 56:3

1. How could remembering Psalm 56:3 help Sarah with her fear?
2. When could Psalm 56:3 help you, too?
3. Memorize Psalm 56:3.

Talking with God

Dear heavenly Father, when I start to feel afraid, help me to trust completely in You. Amen.

Try This!

As a family, make a creepy crawly poster. Draw or glue pictures of all the things that frighten you onto a large piece of paper. Set aside a night or two to study as much as you can about each one. Read an encyclopedia entry or books from the library, watch a video about it, or talk to someone who doesn't share your fear.

If Sarah had done this, she would have learned that spiders are often harmless and always a fascinating part of God's creation.

23 The Birthday Surprise

Eddie had wanted a new bike ever since he had outgrown his old one. The bike he wanted had shiny silver handlebars and a black leather seat. The body was glittery red with white racing stripes along the sides.

Eddie dreamed about the bike at night. He daydreamed about it every time he walked past a certain store, too.

When Eddie's birthday rolled around, he knew just what he'd get. He'd even told his friends, "Wait till you see my new birthday bike!"

After supper, Eddie blew out the candles on his cake. He saw Mom slip out of the room to get his present. He could hardly wait for her to wheel the bike into the room.

But when Mom returned, she held a small, square package out to him. "Here, Eddie," she said with a grin. "Happy birthday, son."

Eddie's face fell. Where was his birthday bike?

What Do You Think?

1. What do you think Eddie said when his mom handed him the small package?
2. Have you ever dreamed of a present that never came?
3. How do you think Eddie's mom felt when she saw the disappointed look on his face?
4. Why does God want us to be thankful for everything?

What Does the Bible Say?

Think about all you can praise God for and be glad about. Philippians 4:8b

1. How could remembering Philippians 4:8b help Eddie get over his disappointment?
2. When could Philippians 4:8b help you, too?
3. Memorize Philippians 4:8b.

Talking with God

Dear Lord, help me to think of all I have instead of what I wish I had. Amen.

Try This!

Make a family blessings chart to hang on the wall. If you have non-readers, use magazine pictures rather than words. Add to it every time you think of something for which you are thankful.

24 The Playground Pup

Leslie and Ann could hardly wait for Friday to arrive. Friday was the day they'd planned a picnic with their moms at the park.

"My mom is making potato salad," said Leslie. "I asked her to dump in extra pickles."

"And we're bringing hot dogs and snickerdoodle cookies," said Ann.

The four met at the park. Leslie and Ann fed the ducks while their mothers started the barbecue. The scent of hot dogs drifted across the cool, shady grass.

A shaggy puppy with sad eyes darted across the grass. Before anyone saw him, he'd dragged two hot dogs and the whole bag of snickerdoodles under their picnic table.

When Ann returned a few minutes later, she found the pup lying under the table, full and contented, with her empty cookie bag beside him.

What Do You Think?

1. What do you think Ann did?
2. What can we learn from the way we treat helpless animals?
3. Why do you think God created animals for us to enjoy?

What Does the Bible Say?

Kindness makes a man attractive. Proverbs 19:22a

1. How could remembering Proverbs 19:22a help Ann decide how to treat the puppy?
2. When could Proverbs 19:22a help you, too?
3. Memorize Proverbs 19:22a.

Talking with God

Thank You, God, for creating animals for us to care for. Amen.

Try This!

If you have a family pet, pick a day to celebrate. If appropriate, buy a special treat for your pet, give it extra playtime, and thank God for giving you such a special friend.

If you don't have a pet, call a wildlife rescue organization or local animal shelter to see if you can visit and donate any supplies (such as old newspapers). Or set up a birdbath or bird feeder in your yard. The library has many books on how to make and maintain them.

25 Money, Money Everywhere

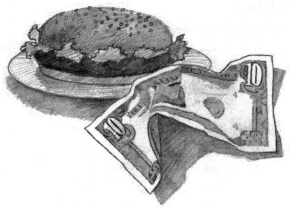

Ramon and his grandfather were spending the afternoon at the county fair.

"Grandpa, look what someone left on the table," cried Ramon. A crumpled ten-dollar bill lay on a table next to the hamburger stand. "Finders keepers, losers weepers," sang Ramon.

Ten dollars! Ramon thought of all the rides he could take for ten dollars. "I'll even have enough to buy us cotton candy," he whispered to Grandpa.

Ramon waited for Grandpa to pat him on the back. He waited for him to say that it was his lucky day.

But Grandpa said nothing. His eyes told Ramon what he ought to do with the money.

What Do You Think?

1. What do you think Ramon did with the ten dollars?
2. Have you ever lost money? How did you feel when you discovered it missing?
3. Is "finders keepers" really a good idea?

What Does the Bible Say?

A good man is known by his truthfulness.
Proverbs 12:17a

1. How could remembering Proverbs 12:17a help Ramon know what to do?
2. When could Proverbs 12:17a help you, too?
3. Memorize Proverbs 12:17a.

Talking with God

Dear heavenly Father, help me to put others' feelings before my own. Amen.

Try This!

Plan and perform a one-act family play in which someone loses something valuable.

26 When I Grow Up

Wendy's Sunday school class had a special assignment.

"We will be in charge of planning the music for our church Christmas program," said Mrs. Dodson. "Who would like to be in charge of the planning committee?"

Nobody moved an inch. Wendy stared at her lap, hoping that Mrs. Dodson would not call on her. Tom played with his pencil. Abby watched a bird on a branch outside the window.

"Wendy?"

The sound of her name startled her. "Yes?" Wendy's voice sounded hoarse and funny.

"How would you like to lead the group?" asked Mrs. Dodson.

Wendy's knees shook at the very thought of being in charge. She could feel her heart thumping against her chest.

In her mind, she wanted to say, *I'll do it when I grow up, but not now.*

"Wendy?" repeated Mrs. Dodson.

What Do You Think?

1. Why do you think Wendy was so afraid of being the leader?
2. What makes a person a good leader? Is everyone naturally good at being a leader?
3. How can God help someone like Wendy? Would it be all right for her to say she would rather not do it at all?

What Does the Bible Say?

For I can do everything God asks me to with the help of Christ who gives me the strength and power.
Philippians 4:13

1. How could remembering Philippians 4:13 help Wendy overcome her fear?
2. When could Philippians 4:13 help you, too?
3. Memorize all or part of Philippians 4:13.

Talking with God

Dear heavenly Father, thank You for encouraging me when I am nervous and afraid. Amen.

Try This!

Take turns talking about something that each person feels he or she "can't" do. Think of ways to encourage that person to try doing it.

27 Caught in the Middle

Todd and his new friend, Olin, were tossing a Frisbee in the empty lot next to the school. It was Olin's first time at the park. He had just moved to town. They'd barely begun their game when Vincent and Scott ran over.

"Let's play two-team Frisbee," said Vincent. "It's more fun that way."

"Get your own Frisbee," snapped Olin.

Todd couldn't help but notice the hurt looks on Vincent's and Scott's faces. He glanced over at Olin, who was holding the Frisbee behind his back like some kind of prize.

"Take a hike," smirked Olin. "Can't you see we're busy?"

Todd felt caught in the middle between two old friends and one new one.

What Do You Think?

1. How do you suppose Todd solved the problem?
2. Why are some people unwilling to share the fun?
3. Have you ever known someone like Olin?
4. What is the best thing to do when you feel "caught in the middle"?

What Does the Bible Say?

You should practice tenderhearted mercy and kindness to others. Colossians 3:12a

1. How could remembering Colossians 3:12a help Todd decide how to handle the situation?
2. When could Colossians 3:12a help you, too?
3. Memorize Colossians 3:12a.

Talking with God

Thank You, dear God, for giving me friends to share fun times with. Amen.

Try This!

Plan a family party to which everyone gets to invite a friend. Choose games that everyone can enjoy, and let each person select a special food to serve.

28 Sorrier Than Sorry

Nita had a big problem. Her friend Torey had promised to come over on Saturday to watch a movie. But Torey did not show up on Saturday.

Nita waited an extra half hour, then she finally phoned Torey's house to see what was taking so long.

"Oh, hi, Nita," said Torey's mother. "Torey's at the library with a friend right now. May I have her call you later?"

"Well, uh . . ." stammered Nita, "she was supposed to come over today. We had plans."

"Oh, I see," replied Torey's mother. "Well, she must have forgotten. I'll have her phone you when she gets home at three-thirty."

Three-thirty? Nita was furious! Torey would be gone almost all afternoon. How could she have forgotten their plans?

When Torey returned home from the library, she called Nita. "I'm sorrier than sorry," she said. "I just forgot."

What Do You Think?

1. What do you think Nita said to Torey?
2. Why is forgiveness important to a friendship?
3. Have you ever made plans and then forgotten them?
4. How do you think Torey felt about disappointing Nita?

What Does the Bible Say?

Love is very patient and kind. . . . It does not hold grudges and will hardly even notice when others do it wrong.
I Corinthians 13:4a, 5c

1. How could remembering I Corinthians 13:4a, 5c help Nita decide how to work things out with Torey?
2. When could I Corinthians 13:4a, 5c help you, too?
3. Memorize all or part of I Corinthians 13:4a, 5c.

Talking with God

Dear Lord, thank You for teaching me how to forgive. Thank You for all the times You have forgiven me. Amen.

Try This!

Have a family forgiveness session. Clear up any misunderstandings, and apologize if you have hurt anyone's feelings this week. Vow to try harder to show patience and love for each other.

29 Who Fed Harry?

Harry was the classroom goldfish. He swam in a bowl on a shelf at the back of the room.

Every week, Miss Gates would write the names of five students on the board. Each morning a different one of those students would be responsible for feeding Harry.

On Friday it was Brian's turn. Harry swam happily until mid-afternoon, when he started acting very sleepy and sick.

Somebody had fed Harry too much goldfish food.

"I only gave him two shakes of food," said Brian. "Somebody else must've given him a snack."

Charlie Foster, who sat in the very back row near Harry's bowl, began to squirm. He'd given Harry just a couple of pinches of food at lunchtime.

Brian eyed him suspiciously.

What Do You Think?

1. What do you think Brian said when he saw Charlie Foster acting so nervous?
2. How do you think Brian felt when Harry got sick?
3. Do you think Charlie meant to make Harry sick?
4. Have you ever made a mistake by trying to help?

What Does the Bible Say?

He helps me do what honors him the most. Psalm 23:3b

1. How could remembering Psalm 23:3b help Brian decide what to do?
2. When could Psalm 23:3b help you, too?
3. Memorize Psalm 23:3b.

Talking with God

Thank You, dear Lord, for giving me the courage to admit my mistakes. Help me to act lovingly when others make mistakes, too. Amen.

Try This!

Think of a time when it was very hard for you to say that you were wrong. Share your story with your family.

30 Marcy's Mess

Yvonne and Marcy were sisters. They had shared a bedroom for as long as they could remember.

Yvonne was neat. Marcy was a clutterer. Yvonne cleaned her side of the room every afternoon. Marcy hid most of her toys and spare socks under the bed.

One day Marcy wasn't feeling well. *I'll get Yvonne to feel sorry for me,* she thought. *Maybe I can even get her to clean my side of the room.*

Marcy laid a hand on her forehead and moaned. "My head is killing me," she told Yvonne. "And my throat is scratchy and sore."

Yvonne watched Marcy toss and turn. She heard her moaning and groaning until she could stand it no more.

Yvonne started cleaning Marcy's side of the room, too. In fact, she was doing such a good job, Marcy began to feel guilty.

What Do You Think?

1. What do you suppose Marcy did next?
2. Was it fair for Marcy to trick her sister?
3. Have you known anyone like Marcy, who avoids his or her share of the work?
4. What would you say to someone like Marcy?

What Does the Bible Say?

Don't act thoughtlessly, but try to find out and do whatever the Lord wants you to. Ephesians 5:17

1. How could remembering Ephesians 5:17 help Marcy decide what to do next?
2. When could Ephesians 5:17 help you, too?
3. Memorize all or part of Ephesians 5:17.

Talking with God

Help me, dear God, to do my best with the chores that belong to me. Amen.

Try This!

Make a list of family chores that need to be done each week. Rotate chores so everyone has a chance to do each task.

Sharing chores will help everyone to better understand and appreciate each other's responsibilities.

31 Make Room for Robbie

Paul and Blaine lived on the same street. They had been best friends since kindergarten. One summer evening, Paul planned to meet Blaine at the neighborhood playground.

When he arrived, Paul found Blaine sitting on the grass with someone new.

"This is Robbie," said Blaine. "He just moved here from Texas."

Paul sized up Robbie. "Hi," he said quietly.

Blaine sprang to his feet. "Let's climb the ropes," he said and raced across the playground with Robbie following close behind.

Paul had to run extra fast to keep up with them.

"Want to crawl through the tunnels?" asked Paul.

Blaine shook his head. "Not today," he said. "I promised Robbie we'd play ball."

"Thanks a lot, Blaine," snapped Paul. "I might as well go home."

What Do You Think?

1. Why do you think Paul was so upset?
2. Do you think Paul and Robbie ever became friends?
3. Why is it sometimes hard to share a best friend?
4. Describe what makes your best friend so special.

What Does the Bible Say?

Love is . . . never jealous or envious. I Corinthians 13:4

1. How would wanting to follow I Corinthians 13:4 help Paul change his mind about Robbie?
2. When could I Corinthians 13:4 help you, too?
3. Memorize I Corinthians 13:4.

Talking with God

Thank You, dear heavenly Father, for giving me all kinds of good friends. Amen.

Try This!

Design your own friendship greeting cards. Send them to your friends to let them know how much you appreciate them.

32 A Way to Help Hannah

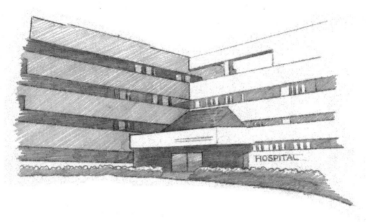

Hannah's grandmother was very ill. Hannah visited the hospital every afternoon after school. And every day, Hannah came away sadder than the day before.

"Don't worry, Hannah," said her friend Jesse. "Your grandmother will be all right. You'll see."

Hannah tried to believe it, but in her heart she still worried.

On Sunday Hannah talked to her Sunday school teacher, Mrs. White. "I don't know how to stop worrying," she said. "I love my grandmother so much."

"I know how you feel," said Mrs. White. She gave Hannah a big hug. "There is a way to help, and I think we should all begin here today."

What Do You Think?

1. What do you suppose Mrs. White was talking about?
2. Have you ever prayed for someone who was sick? What happened?
3. What could Hannah pray for concerning her grandmother?

What Does the Bible Say?

When I pray for you, my heart is full of joy. Philippians 1:4

1. How could remembering Philippians 1:4 help Hannah solve her worrying problem?
2. When could Philippians 1:4 help you, too?
3. Memorize Philippians 1:4.

Talking with God

Dear Lord, thank You for hearing all of my prayers. Help me to understand Your "no" and "wait" answers as well as Your "yes" answers. Amen.

Try This!

Make a family prayer list. Take a few minutes every day to pray for your friends and loved ones who are sick, lonely, or worried. Ask God to bless and help them. Ask Him how you could be part of His answers.

33 Where's Whitney?

Whitney Young was not at school on Monday and Tuesday. Her friends were worried about her.

"Maybe she moved away without telling anybody," suggested Frankie.

"Maybe she's got the flu," said Gina. "My uncle had it last week."

"Maybe she's just tired of school," said April. "I sure feel that way sometimes."

April folded a jumbo piece of blue construction paper in half. She selected ten brightly colored markers.

"I've got an idea," she told the others. "Let's make a surprise for Whitney."

"I could deliver it," said Frankie. "I walk right by her house on my way home from school."

"And I have a piece of gum we could give her, too," added Gina.

What Do You Think?

1. What do you think April and her classmates were planning to make?
2. Have you ever received a surprise when you were absent from school?
3. Think of some ways that God shows His love for you.

What Does the Bible Say?

So encourage each other to build each other up.
I Thessalonians 5:11a

1. How could remembering I Thessalonians 5:11a give the children ideas about how to help Whitney?
2. When could I Thessalonians 5:11a help you, too?
3. Memorize all or part of I Thessalonians 5:11a.

Talking with God

Dear God, thank You for being so loving and kind. Amen.

Try This!

Write a family thank-You card to God. Thank Him for all He has done for you.

34 A Breakfast Picnic

It was a lovely spring morning. Debbie was the first one out of bed. She loved waking up before anyone else. In fact, Daddy had nicknamed her "Early Bird."

The front yard was bathed in yellow sunlight. A mother bird chirped a sweet song to her hungry babies.

Today feels like a picnic day, thought Debbie. But then she thought of what Mom would probably say.

First things first! That's what Mom always said. Debbie had plenty of chores to complete before she could even think about eating a picnic lunch under the old apple tree.

There were eggs to gather and lambs to feed. Living on a farm meant chores that never seemed to end.

Debbie stepped outside and hugged herself in the cool, crisp air. *What about a breakfast picnic?* she thought. *I could be back before nine if I hurry. Mom and Daddy would never even miss me!*

What Do You Think?

1. Do you think Debbie should sneak off for a breakfast picnic? Why or why not?
2. What would the world be like if nobody did chores on time?
3. Name some chores that need to be done on time.

What Does the Bible Say?

The work of the godly will flourish. Proverbs 14:11b

1. How could remembering Proverbs 14:11b help Debbie decide what to do?
2. When could Proverbs 14:11b help you, too?
3. Memorize Proverbs 14:11b.

Talking with God

Thank You, dear God, for giving me a healthy body so I can help my family. Amen.

Try This!

Think of a family project that needs to be done, such as cleaning the garage. Decide how you will split the work load.

When the job is completed, plan a breakfast picnic together. It will be fun, whether it's indoors or out!

35 Don't Forget

Derrick and his older brother, Kevin, were planning a day at the lake.

"We'll be able to leave sooner if you pack while I'm at work. Here's a list of reminders," Kevin told him. "Make sure you check the list so we don't forget anything."

"Yeah," added Derrick, "like you forgot our lunch last time!"

Derrick gathered all the items on the list. When Kevin got home from work, everything was waiting in the driveway.

"This is great! Sure you got everything?" Kevin asked.

"As sure as sure can be," nodded Derrick.

Kevin loaded the ice chest, water jug, and tackle box into his pickup. He tossed in their jackets and an extra pair of shoes, too.

When they were halfway to the lake, Kevin asked, "Hey, Derrick, you did remember to bring that new package of fishing hooks, didn't you?"

The hooks! Derrick had forgotten them. But if he told Kevin the truth, he'd never hear the end of it.

What Do You Think?

1. How do you suppose Derrick answered Kevin?
2. Do you think Derrick checked the list carefully, the way Kevin expected him to?
3. Are you careful to follow through when you're asked to do something?
4. Is it always best to tell the truth? Why or why not?

What Does the Bible Say?

Take a lesson from the ants, you lazy fellow. Learn from their ways and be wise! Proverbs 6:6

1. How could remembering Proverbs 6:6 help Derrick do a good job?
2. When could Proverbs 6:6 help you, too?
3. Memorize all or part of Proverbs 6:6.

Talking with God

Dear heavenly Father, please help me to be faithful in all my duties. Amen.

Try This!

Write an IOU for a "bonus chore" you'd like to do for the family this week. Write down the day you plan to do it, and make sure you get it done on time.

36 Sitting up Front

On a gorgeous morning in September, the Cooper family piled into their van. The weatherman had predicted a sunny, mild day. They were headed for the zoo.

"How come she gets to sit up front again?" complained Andrew.

"Because I'm older," glared Vanessa.

"Daaaad!" wailed Andrew. "It's not fair. 'Nessa always gets to sit up front."

Dad thought for a moment. "He's right," he told Vanessa. "You've sat up front the last four or five times. Don't you think it's Andrew's turn today?"

"But Dad," protested Vanessa, "I'm older. That ought to be good for something!"

Dad gave her a look that said, "Use your good judgment." Vanessa hated making decisions like that.

What Do You Think?

1. Why do you think it was a hard decision for Vanessa?
2. Have you ever insisted on having your way, even though you knew it wasn't fair?
3. Why do you think sitting up front was such a big deal to Andrew?

What Does the Bible Say?

Happy are those who strive for peace. Matthew 5:9a

1. How could remembering Matthew 5:9a have helped Vanessa decide what to do?
2. When could Matthew 5:9a help you, too?
3. Memorize Matthew 5:9a.

Talking with God

Help me, Lord, to treat others as fairly as I would like to be treated. Amen.

Try This!

If sitting "up front" is a big deal at your house, try making a schedule. Post it on the visor of the family car and check it before choosing seats for each family outing.

37 Shhh!

Tuesday was Vonnie's favorite day to visit the city library. All of her friends went on Tuesdays, too. There they would meet in a carpeted, sunken area called "the pit."

They'd read a little and talk a lot. Sometimes their chattering earned them a scolding from the librarian, Mrs. Cummings.

"Shhh!" Mrs. Cummings would hiss, leaning over the railing above the pit. "Keep your voices down. This is a library, not a racetrack!"

Most of the kids would just roll their eyes, then return to their reading or studying. Even though she sounded gruff, they liked Mrs. Cummings. She was always willing to help them and knew the answer to almost any question.

One Tuesday, Vonnie told the other kids, "Mrs. Cummings is too strict. She acts like she's the chief of police or something." Vonnie thought for a moment, then added, "I wonder what she would do if we kept right on talking."

A second later, Mrs. Cummings was standing once again at the railing, peering down into the pit. "Shhh!"

What Do You Think?

1. What do you suppose Vonnie did next?
2. Do you think Mrs. Cummings was being too strict?
3. What would a library be like if everyone talked as loudly as they liked?
4. What kind of an example was Vonnie being to her friends?

What Does the Bible Say?

Keep a close watch on all you do and think. Stay true to what is right and God will bless you and use you to help others. I Timothy 4:16

1. How could remembering I Timothy 4:16 help Vonnie decide what to do next?
2. When could I Timothy 4:16 help you, too?
3. Memorize all or part of I Timothy 4:16.

Talking with God

Dear God, help me to treat others with respect, even if I disagree with their rules. Amen.

Try This!

Read a few passages from the Book of Leviticus. Although most of the rules for the Israelites make little sense to us today, each one was taken seriously during Bible times. Discuss some of the rules that Jesus has lovingly given us to live by.

38 Too Busy to Picnic?

The annual Sunday school picnic was scheduled for Saturday. Kyle's whole family was planning to attend—all except for Kyle, who decided that he was too busy.

"What? Not going to the picnic?" questioned Dad. "Why not, Kyle?"

"Uh . . . I need to finish my model plane," stammered Kyle.

"Well, your model plane can just wait," huffed Mom. "There's plenty of time to finish it later."

". . . and I also promised to play ball on Saturday with Scott," added Kyle.

"Invite him to the picnic," said Dad. "There's plenty of room to play ball there."

Kyle made a sour face. "I just don't feel like going, that's all!" he shouted and stomped out of the kitchen.

"You'll be missing some good food," said Mom, who followed him to his room. "Besides, Kyle, we have such good fellowship at the picnic every year."

Who needs fellowship? moped Kyle. *Not me—that's for sure.*

What Do You Think?

1. Why do you suppose Kyle wanted to avoid the picnic?
2. What is so special about being with other Christians?
3. Do you think Kyle should have to go to the picnic? Why or why not?
4. What is Christian fellowship? What are some of your favorite times of fellowship at your church?

What Does the Bible Say?

Continue to love each other with true brotherly love. Hebrews 13:1

1. How could remembering Hebrews 13:1 help Kyle think through his attitude about the picnic?
2. When could Hebrews 13:1 help you, too?
3. Memorize all or part of Hebrews 13:1.

Talking with God

Thank You, dear Lord, for my church family. Amen.

Try This!

Think about some of the church gatherings your family has attended. Share what you liked best about them. Discuss why Christians are like "family."

39 The Marbles That Disappeared

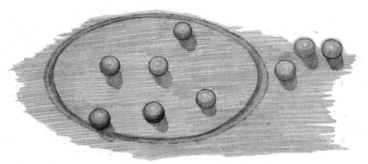

Billy and his best pal, Ryan, wanted to play a game of marbles.

"I can't find my marbles," grumbled Ryan. "My sister borrowed them, and I haven't seen them since."

"No problem," Billy told him. "I'll ask if I can borrow Skip's."

Skip was Billy's brother. He never complained much and always loaned Billy his bag of steelies and cat's-eyes.

"Take good care of them," cautioned Skip.

Billy and Ryan played marbles until their moms called them in for lunch. Billy thought about Skip's reminder to take good care of his marbles. He'd only be gone for a few minutes, though.

"We can leave them set up while we eat," said Billy. "Nobody will bother them."

When Billy and Ryan returned, every last marble was gone! Even the red bag had been taken.

"Oh, boy, are you in trouble now," moaned Ryan.

"I ought to just tell Skip that I left them in his room when we were through playing," said Billy.

What Do You Think?

1. Do you think Billy followed through with his plan to lie to Skip?
2. Have you ever carelessly lost something that belonged to someone else? What happened?
3. What can we learn from this story?

What Does the Bible Say?

The upright are directed by their honesty. Proverbs 11:5a

1. How could remembering Proverbs 11:5a help Billy decide what to say to Skip?
2. When could Proverbs 11:5a help you, too?
3. Memorize Proverbs 11:5a.

Talking with God

God, help me to be honest even when it hurts. Amen.

Try This!

Make up five or six "What would you do if. . . ?" situations to discuss. Choose situations that emphasize honesty.

40 Why Try?

Tenisha received a phone call one Thursday evening. It was Mrs. Washington, who owned the dress shop on Fourth Street.

"Hello, Tenisha," said Mrs. Washington. "How would you like to be in our spring fashion show on Saturday? I have six beautiful dresses I'd like you to model."

"Me—in a fashion show?" laughed Tenisha. "I don't think so, Mrs. Washington."

"Now, it's nothing to be nervous about, dear," explained Mrs. Washington. "You'll simply be walking across a stage, turning once or twice, and exiting the other side."

Tenisha thought her heart would thump right out of her chest. It made her light-headed just thinking of walking across a stage in front of all those people.

"Why try if I know I wouldn't enjoy it?" asked Tenisha.

Mrs. Washington said nothing for a moment. "Well, dear," she said sweetly, "give it some thought, will you? You'll get to keep one of the dresses just for being in the show. I'll call you back tomorrow afternoon for your answer."

What Do You Think?

1. Do you think Tenisha decided to take part in the fashion show?
2. Why do you suppose Tenisha was so shy? Are you shy about performing in front of groups?
3. Tenisha wasn't sure she could be a model. How do you feel about trying something new?
4. What kinds of things do you most enjoy doing?

What Does the Bible Say?

For I cried to him and he answered me! He freed me from all my fears. Psalm 34:4

1. How could remembering Psalm 34:4 help Tenisha calm her fears?
2. When could Psalm 34:4 help you, too?
3. Memorize all or part of Psalm 34:4.

Talking with God

Dear God, help me to believe that I can do anything with Your help. Amen.

Try This!

Think of an experience that you're afraid to try. Talk about all the reasons why you feel you "can't" do it. Then have your family tell you all the reasons why they believe you can do it.

41 Crybaby

A rowdy group of boys was huddled in a circle at the park when Shawn walked up. Shawn could see a younger boy sitting on the grass in the middle of the group.

The boy was crying.

"Whatsa matter?" teased a tall, lanky kid. "You a crybaby or what?"

The younger boy sniffed but did not answer.

A chant began, first softly, then louder and louder. "Crybaby! Crybaby! Crybaby!"

Shawn tried to walk away. He wanted nothing to do with the group of mean boys.

But something inside of him drew him closer. And when the sobbing little boy in the middle looked up at him with tears streaming down his face, Shawn knew he had to do something.

What Do You Think?

1. What do you suppose Shawn did?
2. Have you ever tried to help someone who was being teased?
3. Why do you think someone would try to hurt somebody's feelings?
4. What is the meaning of the word *compassion*?

What Does the Bible Say?

And those who are peacemakers will plant seeds of peace and reap a harvest of goodness. James 3:18

1. How could remembering James 3:18 give Shawn the courage to do what he knows is right?
2. When could James 3:18 help you, too?
3. Memorize all or part of James 3:18.

Talking with God

Dear Lord, show me ways that I can be a peacemaker for You. Amen.

Try This!

Think of somebody you know who is having a hard time making friends. Ask God to show you how to be a friend to him or her.

42 Who's There?

Elisa and her family were staying at a cabin in the mountains for a whole week. One morning while Elisa slept, her parents decided to go fishing at a creek that ran behind the cabin. They stepped out into the chilly mountain air and locked the door behind them.

When they returned an hour later, they discovered that neither of them had taken a key.

"Elisa?" called Dad. "Wake up. Mom and I need to come in."

Elisa sat up in bed and rubbed her eyes. What were Mom and Dad doing outside so early in the morning?

"How do I know it's really you?" called Elisa. "What color are your eyes, mister?"

"Purple polka-dotted," kidded Dad. "Now let me in, please."

Elisa still couldn't be sure it was Mom and Dad. It sounded like them, but she had no real proof. And Mom had taught her never to open the door to strangers.

What Do You Think?

1. Do you think Elisa finally opened the door?
2. How would you describe trust?
3. Why is trust important between family members?
4. Can we really trust in a God we cannot see?

What Does the Bible Say?

This I declare, that he alone is my refuge, my place of safety; he is my God, and I am trusting him. Psalm 91:2

1. How could Psalm 91:2 help Elisa keep calm enough to make a safe decision?
2. When could Psalm 91:2 help you, too?
3. Memorize all or part of Psalm 91:2.

Talking with God

Dear heavenly Father, help me to trust in You even though I cannot see You. Amen.

Try This!

Name some invisible parts of creation that we believe in, even though we cannot see them. (Examples: gravity, wind)

43 The Two Missing Words

Tyrone stood in a long line at a hot-dog stand.

"They make the world's best chili dogs here," said his Uncle Darren. "You'll be glad you waited."

Tyrone and Uncle Darren watched a man and lady grow impatient and drop out of line. They saw a pair of teenagers wait until they'd reached the sixth place from the window. All of a sudden one of them glanced at his watch and growled, "I'm outta here."

A little boy in front of Tyrone waited quietly. But when the lady at the window handed him a hot dog, he grabbed it out of her hands without saying a word. She slid his soft drink across the counter.

"I need a straw," he demanded as he put his money on the counter.

The lady gave him a straw, then raised her eyebrows and waited. The boy turned away rudely.

"That little guy needs to learn the two missing words," whispered Uncle Darren.

What Do You Think?

1. What two words was Uncle Darren talking about?
2. Why is it so important to say "thank you"?
3. Does God like to hear us express our thanks to Him, too? Why?

What Does the Bible Say?

It is good to say, "Thank you" to the Lord. Psalm 92:1a

1. How could remembering Psalm 92:1a help Tyrone keep the two missing words on his lips?
2. When could Psalm 92:1a help you, too?
3. Memorize Psalm 92:1a.

Talking with God

Thank You, God, for always taking good care of me. Amen.

Try This!

Buy a box of thank-you notes. Write thank-yous to friends and teachers who make your life richer.

44 Jason's Welcome Wagon

A shiny red wagon sat in a corner of Jason McCoy's garage. The wagon was a gift from his grandparents.

Jason could remember the day he received the wagon. He tore open the shiny birthday paper and hollered with delight, "It's just what I wanted. Thanks!"

Jason had used his wagon to transport his puppy, Rollo. Sometimes he hauled leaves in it or his sister, Mimi. And one day God had a special use for it, too.

Jason was playing on his front step when he heard a CRASH! A neighbor lady had dropped two bags of groceries on the sidewalk. Both bags had ripped wide open.

"Oh dear!" Jason heard her say. "How will I ever get these home?"

And that's when God gave Jason a super idea.

What Do You Think?

1. What do you think Jason did to help the lady?
2. How could you use one of your special possessions for God?
3. Do you know what the word *stewardship* means? (Look it up in the dictionary if you aren't sure.) Are you being a good steward?

What Does the Bible Say?

All the believers were of one heart and mind, and no one felt that what he owned was his own; everyone was sharing. Acts 4:32

1. How could remembering Acts 4:32 help Jason be a good steward of all God has given him?
2. When could Acts 4:32 help you, too?
3. Memorize all or part of Acts 4:32.

Talking with God

Help me find special ways, dear God, to use all You have given me. Amen.

Try This!

Do you have a possession that could help others? (Possible ideas are a sled, car, bicycle, computer, even crayons.) How could you use it to help others? Decide upon one special task that you will do this week for God.

45 A Real Friend

Twila and her dad were shopping for a Mother's Day gift.

"Let's look at perfume," suggested Twila. "Mom loves perfume."

They smelled every bottle of perfume at the display counter. Twila tried so many testers, her wrist smelled like a garden of flowers.

"Which one shall we buy?" asked Dad.

Twila worked her way around the long, mirrored counter. When she reached the corner, she glanced up to see a friend from school.

"Oh, hi, Marlene," called Twila. "Shopping for Mother's Day?"

Marlene pulled one hand quickly out of her purse. She looked like she wanted to faint. Twila suddenly realized what she was seeing. Marlene was stealing one of the sample perfume testers!

Twila's heart sank. She didn't know what to do or say next.

What Do You Think?

1. What do you think Twila decided to do?
2. Would a real friend ignore her friend's theft?
3. What would you say if you caught a friend stealing?

What Does the Bible Say?

Share each other's troubles and problems, and so obey our Lord's command. Galatians 6:2

1. How could remembering Galatians 6:2 help Twila decide what to do?
2. When could Galatians 6:2 help you, too?
3. Memorize all or part of Galatians 6:2.

Talking with God

Thank You, God, for giving me courage to speak up when it's hard. Amen.

Try This!

Have each family member think of a situation that would require a lot of courage. Take turns acting out how you would solve it.

◤46◥ Please Don't Tell

Alvaro Gomez had a special anniversary surprise in store for his parents. Neighborhood friends were going to bring food for a backyard potluck. Alvaro had arranged music, games, and decorations. It would be a party for his parents to remember always.

Alvaro's friend Susan would be at the party. Her parents were bringing the special cake.

"Please don't tell my mother or father about the party," Alvaro told Susan. "I want them to be surprised."

But the next day, Susan stopped to talk to Alvaro and his mom as they worked in the yard. "It's such a pretty day," Susan told Mrs. Gomez. "I sure hope we have nice weather for your party."

Alvaro couldn't believe what he was hearing.

What Do You Think?

1. What do you suppose Alvaro said to Susan?
2. Have you ever slipped and ruined a surprise? How did you feel afterwards?
3. Do you think Alvaro forgave Susan for telling his mother about the party? Why or why not?
4. Can you trust God with your deepest secrets?

What Does the Bible Say?

God delights in those who keep their promises.
Proverbs 12:22a

1. How could remembering Proverbs 12:22a have helped Susan be extra careful not to spoil the surprise?
2. When could Proverbs 12:22a help you, too?
3. Memorize Proverbs 12:22a.

Talking with God

Help me, dear Heavenly Father, to always be a trustworthy friend. Amen.

Try This!

Make a list of all the people you can trust with your secrets. Take a few minutes to thank God for each one. Ask Him to make you a trustworthy friend, too.

47 Close to Home

Shantel's great-grandmother had been in the hospital for more than a week. Every evening after supper, Shantel and her parents visited her. Sometimes Shantel took fresh flowers from their garden.

And every evening, they found Great Grandmother singing praises to God. "God is taking good care of me," she always told them. But her words only confused Shantel.

How could God be taking good care of her if she felt so terrible?

One evening Great Grandma's room was quiet. She pulled Shantel close and whispered, "I'm going home soon!" She smiled sweetly at Shantel and squeezed her hand.

Shantel smiled back nervously. She knew that Great Grandma was not well enough to go home yet. In fact, she looked like she might have to stay in the hospital for a long, long time.

Later that night as Shantel lay in bed, she thought about what Great Grandma had said. And she began to understand why she had smiled so peacefully.

What Do You Think?

1. What did Shantel suddenly realize?
2. Why could Great Grandma praise God while feeling so sick?
3. Why did Great Grandma call heaven "home"?

What Does the Bible Say?

There are many homes up there where my Father lives, and I am going to prepare them for your coming. When everything is ready, then I will come and get you, so that you can always be with me where I am. John 14:2, 3

1. How could remembering John 14:2, 3 help Shantel when her great-grandmother does go "home"?
2. When could John 14:2, 3 help you, too?
3. Memorize all or part of John 14:2, 3.

Talking with God

Thank You, God, for preparing a wonderful new home for everyone who loves You! Amen.

Try This!

Make a list of some of your family's favorite places. Talk about why you like each one. Now take a few moments to think about heaven. Heaven will be even more wonderful than our favorite place here on earth. Jesus will be there, and we'll live forever in perfect happiness.

48 Where the Biggest Berries Grow

Emma and Patsy had been friends ever since they were toddlers. Wherever Emma went, Patsy followed. Whenever Patsy had a problem, Emma helped her find a solution.

One day Emma and Patsy decided to gather a bucketful of blackberries.

"Don't go far, Emma," cautioned her mother. "There's poison oak in the woods."

Emma and Patsy picked berries in the patch behind Emma's house. But there didn't seem to be many berries left on those bushes.

"The biggest berries grow on bushes in that big clearing near the lake," said Patsy.

Emma remembered her mother's warning. But one peek in the bucket told her that they had a long way to go before it would be full.

What Do You Think?

1. Do you think Emma took Patsy's advice or her mother's?
2. Have you ever had a friend who encouraged you to disobey your mom or dad?
3. Is a bucketful of berries worth the price of disobeying?

What Does the Bible Say?

What a blessing this has been to me—to constantly obey.
Psalm 119:56

1. How could remembering Psalm 119:56 help Patsy to decide what to do?
2. When could Psalm 119:56 help you, too?
3. Memorize Psalm 119:56.

Talking with God

Dear Lord, help me to turn away from anything or anyone that would tempt me to disobey. Amen.

Try This!

Take a car ride and see how many different road safety signs you can spot. What would our highways be like if we had no road signs?

In much the same way, God gives us parents who love us and want us to have a safe, happy life. That's why they give us rules we must follow. And what's more, when we break Mom or Dad's rules, we are automatically breaking God's rules, because God has placed children in their parents' care.

49 Push or Pull?

Jonathan's family was moving into a new house. Moving meant lots of sorting, packing, carrying, and stacking.

"If each of us does our part, the move will go smoothly," said Dad.

Jonathan packed his clothes and toys into cardboard boxes. He stacked the boxes by his bedroom door for the movers to collect.

"I'm done," he called.

"Oh, no, you're not," laughed Dad. "Follow me."

Dad led Jonathan straight to his little brother's room. "Shane needs some help with his packing, too," said Dad.

Jonathan's face grew red and angry. "But Shane never has to finish anything he starts!" he grumbled. "He acts like he's helpless."

Three-year-old Shane looked sadly at his big brother. He pointed to a large box that needed to be moved out of the way.

"You want to push, or you want to pull, Jon'than?"

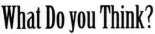

What Do you Think?

1. Do you think Jonathan had a right to be upset?
2. How do you think Shane felt when Jonathan didn't want to help him?
3. Do you ever feel like you have too much work to do?
4. Can you think of someone who once helped you without being asked?

What Does the Bible Say?

A brother is born to help in time of need.
Proverbs 17:17b

1. How could Proverbs 17:17b help Jonathan change his mind about helping Shane?
2. When could Proverbs 17:17b help you, too?
3. Memorize Proverbs 17:17b. (Proverbs 17:17a was memorized for devotional nine.)

Talking with God

Help me, dear God, to look for ways to help my loved ones. Amen.

Try This!

Try doing a chore (such as washing dishes) with one hand held behind your back. See how hard it is? Talk about how much more can be accomplished when people work together. Choose a partner, and think of a project the two of you can accomplish together.

50 Erika's White Easter Egg

Erika loved Easter more than any other holiday.

Easter meant a pretty new dress to wear to church, a basketful of goodies, and lots of bunny decorations at the mall.

It also meant getting to color Easter eggs at Grandma's house. "I want this one to be spotted," Erika told Grandma. "And this one will be pink and green striped."

Together, Grandma and Erika colored eighteen eggs. When they had finished, Erika reached for a white egg that Grandma had already set in the middle of the basket.

"Look, Grandma," she said, "we forgot to color this one."

"Oh, no, honey," Grandma replied with a grin. "That one's supposed to be white. The white eggs stands for what happens inside of us when we invite Jesus into our hearts."

What Do You Think?

1. What do you think Grandma meant?
2. Does your family color Easter eggs? Have you ever left one egg white?
3. How can we show God how much we love Him?

What Does the Bible Say?

For God loved the world so much that he gave his only Son so that anyone who believes in him shall not perish but have eternal life. John 3:16

1. How could remembering John 3:16 help Erika understand the true meaning of Easter?
2. When could John 3:16 help you, too?
3. Memorize all or part of John 3:16.

Talking with God

Thank You, God, for loving me so much. Help me to show others Your love. Amen.

Try This!

Make a batch of sugar cookie dough. Roll out the dough, and cut it into egg-shaped cookies. Frost all but one in bright colors; frost the last cookie with plain white icing. Arrange the cookies in a pretty basket, and deliver the basket to a shut-in, along with a homemade card. Be ready to explain why the one "egg" is white.

51 The Count-Your-Blessings Quilt

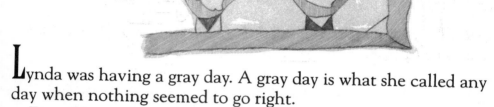

Lynda was having a gray day. A gray day is what she called any day when nothing seemed to go right.

First she accidentally broke one of her glass animal figurines. Later, her cat, Stormy, slipped out the back door and ran away.

"I can't find Stormy anywhere," cried Lynda. "He'll probably never come home."

Lynda laid on her bed and moped. She traced around the fabric squares of the quilt that Mom had made for her last Christmas. Each square represented a special memory of friendships, accomplishments, birthdays, and pets. Even Stormy had a square on Lynda's quilt.

"It's a count-your-blessings quilt," she remembered Mom saying.

Lynda's fingers traced the outline of a pair of folded hands. The hands were folded in prayer.

Even though it felt like a gray day, the quilt reminded Lynda of something she could do to make it better.

What Do You Think?

1. What do you suppose Lynda did next?
2. How can praying make a gray day better?
3. Do we need to be in a special place to pray? Why or why not?
4. When was the last time you counted your blessings?

What Does the Bible Say?

All day long I'll praise and honor you, O God, for all that you have done for me. Psalm 71:8

1. How could remembering Psalm 71:8 help Lynda on her gray days?
2. When could Psalm 71:8 help you, too?
3. Memorize all or part of Psalm 71:8.

Talking with God

Thank You, God, for always being there to talk to. Amen.

Try This!

Cut several strips of colored paper for each family member. On each strip, write or draw something for which you are thankful. Put all the strips in an empty bag or shoe box.

The next time you are experiencing a gray day like Lynda's, reach in and pick out a strip of paper. It will remind you of the way God continues to bless you.

52 The Very Best Christmas Gift

Stuart awoke early on Christmas morning. The house was dim and still. Everyone else was sleeping soundly.

Stuart stood before the six-foot tree in the corner of the living room. It was the prettiest Christmas tree he had ever seen.

"There must be three zillion presents!" he whispered to himself. And while the tree lights twinkled, Stuart counted every package which bore his name.

One tiny package felt as light as a snowflake. Stuart shook it and squeezed it. When he couldn't stand the suspense, he opened one end of the paper and peeked inside the box.

A large capital *J*, cut from shiny gold foil, lay inside.

What a strange present, thought Stuart.

What Do You Think?

1. What do you suppose the J stood for?
2. If Jesus is the best Christmas gift of all, why is it easy to forget Him at Christmas?
3. What special thing does your family do to celebrate Jesus' birthday?

What Does the Bible Say?

"And she will have a Son, and you shall name him Jesus (meaning 'Savior'), for he will save his people from their sins." Matthew 1:21

1. How could remembering Matthew 1:21 help Stuart appreciate the best gift of Christmas?
2. When could Matthew 1:21 help you, too?
3. Memorize all or part of Matthew 1:21.

Talking with God

Thank You, God, for sending me the best Christmas present of all. Amen.

Try This!

Make some foil J's to wrap for special friends this Christmas. Be ready to share the story of Jesus with them.

Scripture Verses

The following pages contain each of the Scripture verses used in this book. You may wish to photocopy these pages, then cut out the appropriate Scripture each week and put it in a visible spot in your home to aid memorization.

1

And all the believers met together constantly and shared everything with each other.

Acts 2:44

2

Children, obey your parents; this is the right thing to do because God has placed them in authority over you.

Ephesians 6:1

3

The Lord hates cheating and delights in honesty.

Proverbs 11:1

4

Don't repay evil for evil. Don't snap back at those who say unkind things about you. Instead, pray for God's help for them, for we are to be kind to others, and God will bless us for it.

I Peter 3:9

5

If you want to know
what God wants you
to do, ask him, and
he will gladly tell you.

James 1:5a

6

A man who refuses to
admit his mistakes can
never be successful.

Proverbs 28:13a

7

Let everyone see that
you are unselfish and
considerate in all you do.

Philippians 4:5a

8

Work hard and with gladness all the time, as though working for Christ, doing the will of God with all your hearts.

Ephesians 6:7

9

A true friend is always loyal.

Proverbs 17:17a

10

But if a person isn't loving and kind, it shows that he doesn't know God— for God is love.

I John 4:8

11

The lazy man is
full of excuses.

Proverbs 22:13a

12

Have two goals: wisdom—
that is, knowing and doing
right—and common sense.

Proverbs 3:21

13

The tongue is a small
thing, but what enormous
damage it can do.

James 3:5a

14

Your own soul is nourished
when you are kind.

Proverbs 11:17a

15

The Lord is fair in everything
he does, and full of kindness.

Psalm 145:17

16

Keep me far from every
wrong; help me,
undeserving as I am,
to obey your laws.

Psalm 119:29

17

If you wait for perfect
conditions, you will never
get anything done.

Ecclesiastes 11:4

18

My protection and
success come from
God alone.

Psalm 62:7a

19

Open my eyes to see
wonderful things
in your Word.

Psalm 119:18

20

Whenever we can
we should always be
kind to everyone.

Galatians 6:10a

21

There is a right time
for everything.

Ecclesiastes 3:1

22

But when I am afraid,
I will put my
confidence in you.

Psalm 56:3

23

Think about all you
can praise God for
and be glad about.

Philippians 4:8b

24

Kindness makes a
man attractive.

Proverbs 19:22a

25

A good man is known
by his truthfulness.

Proverbs 12:17a

26

For I can do everything God asks me to with the help of Christ who gives me the strength and power.

Philippians 4:13

27

You should practice tenderhearted mercy and kindness to others.

Colossians 3:12a

28

Love is very patient and kind. . . . It does not hold grudges and will hardly even notice when others do it wrong.

I Corinthians 13:4a, 5c

29

He helps me do
what honors
him the most.

Psalm 23:3b

30

Don't act thoughtlessly,
but try to find out and
do whatever the
Lord wants you to.

Ephesians 5:17

31

Love is . . . never
jealous or envious.

I Corinthians 13:4

32

When I pray for you,
my heart is full of joy.

Philippians 1:4

33

So encourage each other
to build each other up.

I Thessalonians 5:11a

34

The work of the godly
will flourish.

Proverbs 14:11b

35

Take a lesson from the ants,
you lazy fellow. Learn from
their ways and be wise!

Proverbs 6:6

36

Happy are those who
strive for peace.

Matthew 5:9a

37

Keep a close watch on
all you do and think. Stay
true to what is right and
God will bless you and use
you to help others.

I Timothy 4:16

38

Continue to love
each other with true
brotherly love.

Hebrews 13:1

39

The upright are directed
by their honesty.

Proverbs 11:5a

40

For I cried to him and he
answered me! He freed
me from all my fears.

Psalm 34:4

41

And those who are peacemakers will plant seeds of peace and reap a harvest of goodness.

James 3:18

42

This I declare, that he alone is my refuge, my place of safety; he is my God, and I am trusting him.

Psalm 91:2

43

It is good to say, "Thank you" to the Lord.

Psalm 92:1a

44

All the believers were of one heart and mind, and no one felt that what he owned was his own; everyone was sharing.

Acts 4:32

45

Share each other's troubles and problems, and so obey our Lord's command.

Galatians 6:2

46

God delights in those who keep their promises.

Proverbs 12:22a

47

There are many homes up there where my Father lives, and I am going to prepare them for your coming. When everything is ready, then I will come and get you, so that you can always be with me where I am.
John 14:2, 3

48

What a blessing this has been to me— to constantly obey.

Psalm 119:56

49

A brother is born to help in time of need.

Proverbs 17:17b

50

For God loved the world so much that he gave his only Son so that anyone who believes in him shall not perish but have eternal life.

John 3:16

51

All day long I'll praise and honor you, O God, for all that you have done for me.

Psalm 71:8

52

"And she will have a Son, and you shall name him Jesus (meaning 'Savior'), for he will save his people from their sins."

Matthew 1:21